Written by Nick Farwell, aka CNB Minecraft
Additional material by Don Steer
Edited by Stephanie Milton and Jane Riordan
Designed by Andrea Philpots and Joe Bolder
Illustrations by James Burlinson, Theo Cordner, Joe Bolder, Cubehamster, SethBling,
JL2579, and FVDisco
Production by Louis Harvey and Caroline Hancock
Special thanks to Lydia Winters, Owen Hill, and Junkboy
With thanks to the testing crew: SethBling, Ali, Bella, Jack, Roman, Adam, William,
Issac, and Oscar

◪MOJANG

Published by arrangement with Mojang and Egmont®

Stay safe online. Any website addresses listed in this book are correct at the time
of going to print. However, Scholastic is not responsible for content hosted by third
parties. Please be aware that online content can be subject to change and websites
can contain content that is unsuitable for children. We advise that all children are
supervised when using the Internet.

This book is a work of fiction. Names, characters, places, and incidents are either the
product of the authors' imaginations or are used fictitiously, and any resemblance to
actual persons, living or dead, business establishments, events, or locales is entirely
coincidental.

ISBN 978-0-545-82324-1

15 14 13 12 11 10 9 8 7 6   16 17 18 19 20/0

Printed in China   62
First published 2014
This edition first printing 2015

MINECRAFT

MOJANG

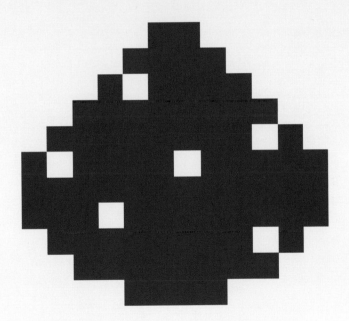

REDSTONE HANDBOOK

CONTENTS

WELCOME TO REDSTONE   6

REDSTONE ESSENTIALS

REDSTONE ORE   8

REDSTONE DUST   10

REDSTONE TORCH   12

REDSTONE REPEATER   13

PISTON   14

STICKY PISTON   15

POWER SOURCES   16

SLIME BLOCKS   20

LIGHTING SYSTEMS   22

PISTON DOORS   24

MINECART STATIONS   28

PULSE SHORTENER   32

TOGGLE FLIP-FLOP   34

CLOCK CIRCUITS   36

REDSTONE CHALLENGES

DELUXE LIGHTING SYSTEM   40

AUTOMATED CHICKEN FARM   44

CLASSIC JEB DOOR   48

LAVA PIT TRAP   52

DUAL SHOT CANNON   56

SUPERCHARGED FIRE ARROW LAUNCHER   60

3X3 PISTON DOOR   64

POTION LAB   70

COMMUNITY CREATIONS

14 FLOOR ELEVATOR BY CUBEHAMSTER   76

COLOR MAP DISPLAY BY SETHBLING   80

SUPER STOPWATCH BY JL2579 & CUBEHAMSTER   82

GOLD RUSH BY CNB   86

ZOMBIE SIEGE BY FVDISCO   90

HINTS AND TIPS   94

USEFUL LINKS   95

WELCOME TO REDSTONE

AN INTRODUCTION TO THE ELECTRIFYING WORLD OF REDSTONE!

Whether you're playing in Survival or Creative mode, redstone is an amazing substance that will open up the immense possibilities of Minecraft. It will enhance your gameplay by teaching you how to connect and control the blocks that make up your world.

Redstone dust and torches were first introduced in Alpha. Repeaters were introduced in the official redstone release Alpha 1.3.1, when it also became possible to obtain redstone by trading with villagers. Witches, who sometimes drop redstone, were introduced in Alpha 1.4.2, followed by pistons in Alpha 1.7. Version 1.5 (aka "The Redstone Update") was released in March 2013.

Since its arrival a huge redstone community has developed, building and sharing creations as diverse as arcade-style games, intricate traps, calculators, and even computers.

NOTE FROM THE AUTHOR: Most serious redstone creators use the PC/Mac Edition, but many of the builds in this book can be created on the Console Edition as well, so go ahead and give them a try!

The first section of this handbook gets you up to speed on the basics of redstone. The second section pushes you to use your new redstone knowledge to complete challenges, and the final section showcases some of the awesome community creations that are out there and gives a little insight into how they work.

SO LET'S GET WIRED UP AND GO CREATE!

REDSTONE ESSENTIALS
ARE YOU READY TO GET FULLY WIRED UP TO REDSTONE?

REDSTONE ORE

Redstone ore is the raw, mineable block from which you get redstone dust. When mined in the PC/Mac Edition with an iron, gold, or diamond pickaxe, each block will drop 4–5 pieces of redstone dust.

WHERE TO FIND IT

Redstone ore is found deep underground, within 1 to 16 blocks of the bedrock layer. Time to get mining, then! Just remember the Number One Rule of Minecraft: Never dig straight down.

REDSTONE ORE

If you're playing in Creative mode, you'll have an infinite supply of redstone at your fingertips. If you're playing in Survival, the easiest way to get to redstone ore is to find a cave system that leads deep underground. This will save you digging your way down by hand and should lead you straight to a nice supply of redstone ore.

ENCHANTING YOUR TOOLS

When mined with an enchanted fortune pickaxe, a block of redstone ore will drop up to 8 pieces of redstone dust.

ENCHANTMENT TABLE RECIPE

Can be used to enchant tools, weapons, and armor in the safety of your own home.

You can enchant your tools on an enchantment table. To craft a table you'll need 4 blocks of obsidian, 2 diamond gems, and 1 book. This is an expensive investment, but an enchanted fortune pickaxe will pay for itself many times over when you start mining redstone, diamond, and emerald.

DID YOU KNOW?

A block of redstone can be used as a power source. See pages 16–17 to find out more!

REDSTONE BLOCK RECIPE

A solid block of redstone can be crafted from 9 pieces of redstone dust.

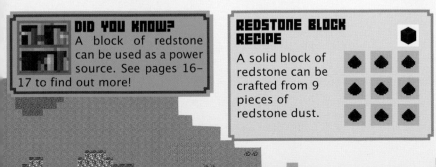

Redstone dust is really powerful stuff and is essential to almost all redstone circuits. Take some time to come to grips with it now, and you'll be glad you did later!

Within a circuit, redstone dust acts like a wire. It carries a redstone signal from a power source to another redstone item, such as a repeater, a piston, or a door.

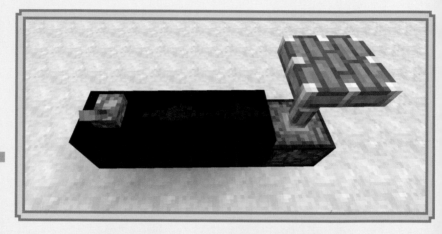

USING REDSTONE DUST

You'll need to place the dust on top of a block, not on the sides or the bottom. Placing several pieces of dust next to each other will create a wire. Simple!

TIP: Remember, redstone dust can't help you until you've given it a power source.

PROPERTIES OF REDSTONE DUST

Redstone dust is pretty smart. You can run it up- and downhill to create a wire without the connection breaking. Just remember that it can't travel vertically more than 1 block at a time.

But, smart as it is, the dust still needs to be told what to do. You need to direct it into the item you want to power. Simply placing an item (e.g. a piston) next to a wire and giving it power won't do the trick. The end of the wire must be pointed at the item you're trying to power.

When the dust receives a signal from a power source, it can send that signal a maximum distance of 15 blocks before it runs out of strength. At that point you can place a repeater at the end of the wire to make the signal last for another 15 blocks. (Turn to page 13 to learn about repeaters.)

THE REDSTONE TORCH

You'll want to familiarize yourself with this handy item. A redstone torch has several uses and, among other things, can act as a power source in a redstone circuit.

HOW A REDSTONE TORCH WORKS

A redstone torch is turned on by default, so when it receives power or a redstone signal it actually turns off. Unlike a lever or a button, you can't switch it on and off by hand.

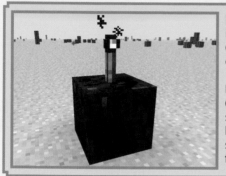

Redstone torches are an essential ingredient for redstone repeaters (see opposite page), redstone comparators, and activator rails.

Redstone torches have a 1 tick (0.1 second) delay when they are switched on or off. When used in long chains, they can cause a few seconds' delay, which you should factor into your calculations.

REDSTONE TORCH RECIPE

You can craft a redstone torch from just a stick and a piece of redstone dust.

TIP: Redstone torches have a light level of 7, which is half the light output of a regular torch. They won't melt ice or snow, and don't try using them as a mob-spawning deterrent or you'll be in for a nasty surprise . . .

 DID YOU KNOW? A tick is an amount of time, and in redstone terms it refers to the time it takes the signal to travel from the power source to the object you are trying to power. A 1-tick delay is 0.1 seconds, a 2-tick delay is 0.2 seconds, and so on.

A redstone repeater is a very useful item. Once you've wired it up the possibilities are endless!

HOW A REPEATER WORKS

A repeater will accept a signal at the back and then push it out of the front with renewed signal strength. For reference, the back of the repeater is the side closest to you when you place it.

REDSTONE REPEATER RECIPE

You can craft a redstone repeater from redstone torches, redstone dust, and stone.

A repeater has several functions, but the two most important are:

1 To increase the distance a redstone-dust wire can send a signal. When added to a circuit, the repeater takes a signal of any strength and refreshes it so that it is repeated at full power (hence its name).

2 To create a delay between receiving the signal and outputting the signal. This is the most important function as the delay is critical to complicated machinery that requires specific timings to work correctly, such as a piston door. The maximum delay that can be created by a repeater is 0.4 seconds, but you can use several repeaters to create longer delays.

By default, the repeater delay is set to 1 tick, but it can be changed to 2, 3, or 4 ticks by hitting the Use Item button when the repeater is in place. You'll notice the torch moves along each time you hit the repeater, signaling that you've changed the tick.

PISTON

Pistons may just be the most revolutionary addition to redstone because they allow redstone circuits to physically move the blocks around you. When given power, a piston can push the blocks in front of it.

PISTON RECIPE

You can craft a piston using wood planks, cobblestone, an iron ingot, and redstone dust.

DID YOU KNOW?

A single piston can push up to 12 blocks at a time, and it can push them in any direction.

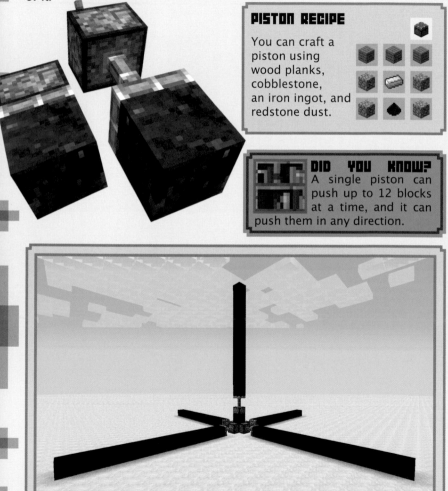

5 pistons, each pushing 12 blocks.

TICKY PISTON

Sticky pistons are often more useful than regular pistons. They can pull a block backward as well as pushing it forward. When a sticky piston receives power it will push a block forward, and when it stops receiving power it will pull the block backward.

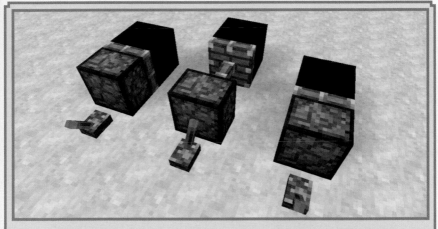

Sticky pistons powered by levers, pulling and pushing blocks.

STICKY PISTON RECIPE

You can craft a sticky piston using a regular piston and a slimeball.

When killed, big slimes divide into small slimes, and small slimes divide into tiny slimes. It's only the tiny slimes that drop slimeballs.

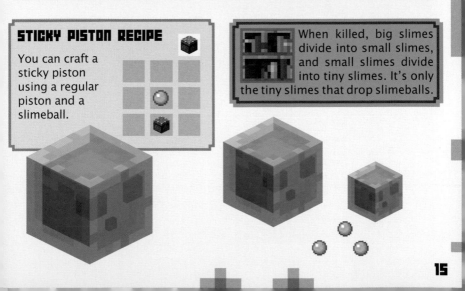

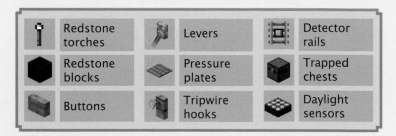

POWER SOURCES

Torches aren't the only power source available to you. There are several other interesting ways to power a circuit. This table shows the different options for powering up with redstone.

🕯	Redstone torches	Levers	Detector rails
⬛	Redstone blocks	Pressure plates	Trapped chests
	Buttons	Tripwire hooks	Daylight sensors

WHAT POWER SOURCES DO

Power sources provide a redstone signal to other redstone items like redstone dust, pistons, and TNT.

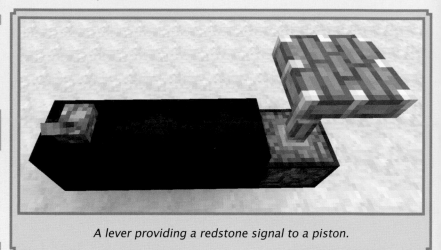

A lever providing a redstone signal to a piston.

USING POWER SOURCES

With the exception of the redstone block, trapped chest, and daylight sensor, a power source needs to be attached to a regular block before it can work.

The power source will then send out a signal for 1 block in all directions except diagonally.

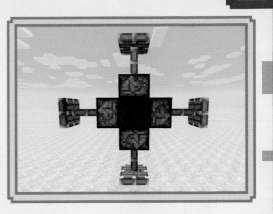

The easiest way to use a power source is to place it next to the item you want to power, since all power sources send power to the blocks next to them. Buttons, levers, pressure plates, trip-wire hooks, and detector rails also power the block to which they are attached, and anything that is next to that block.

TURNING POWER SOURCES ON AND OFF

A lever can be toggled on and off, allowing you much more control over your circuits and machines. The only power source that can't be turned off is a redstone block.

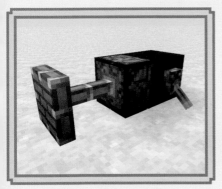

SENDING YOUR REDSTONE SIGNAL IN A SPECIFIC DIRECTION

As you now know, a power source sends out a signal in all directions except diagonally. However, if the power source is next to redstone dust or a repeater, you can use those items to direct it wherever you want it to go.

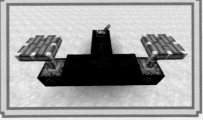

...CONTINUED

We've looked at a few power sources already, but here are some additional power-source recipes that will come in handy for the upcoming challenges!

WOODEN BUTTON

Produces a 1.5-second redstone signal when pressed

Must be attached to a block

Can be activated by arrows (they will keep the button pressed)

STONE BUTTON

Produces a 1-second redstone signal when pressed

Must be attached to a block

Cannot be activated by arrows

Replace the wood with stone for a stone button.

WOODEN PRESSURE PLATE

Produces a 1-second redstone signal (unless constantly pressed down)

Can only be placed on top of a block

Can be activated by a player, animal, monster, minecart, boat, or dropped item

STONE PRESSURE PLATE

Produces a 1-second redstone signal (unless constantly pressed down)

Can only be placed on top of a block

Can only be activated by a player or monster, not dropped items

Replace with stone for a stone pressure plate.

WEIGHTED PRESSURE PLATE

Can only be placed on top of a block

Can only be activated by a dropped item

Produces a 1-second redstone signal (unless constantly pressed down)

Amount of items dropped onto pressure plate increases its redstone signal strength

Replace the iron with gold for a gold-weighted pressure plate.

LEVER

Must be attached to a block

Can be toggled on and off by the player

Produces a constant redstone signal

TRIP-WIRE HOOK

Must have a second trip-wire hook opposite (2 blocks or more away)

Produces a 0.5-second redstone signal (unless constantly pressed down)

Connected with string to the other trip-wire hook

Will react to players, monsters, animals, minecarts, boats, and dropped items

Must be attached to a block

SLIME BLOCKS

Transparent slime blocks have several unique properties making them highly useful blocks. Their addition to the game in 1.8 has opened up a whole new world of piston contraption possibilities.

HOW SLIME BLOCKS WORK

Slime blocks stick to other blocks. So, when pushed or pulled by a piston, they will take the block that they are touching with them.

There are some important things to remember when using slime blocks:

SLIME BLOCK RECIPE

You can craft a slime block from 9 slimeballs, which are dropped by tiny slimes.

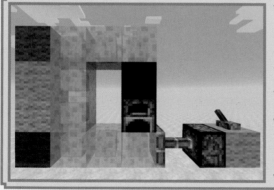

They don't stick to any blocks that can't usually be moved by pistons (e.g. obsidian, hoppers, and furnaces). You can use this property to your advantage — try placing your redstone wire on obsidian so the slime doesn't pick up unwanted blocks as it moves around inside your contraption.

If you push a regular block that is attached to a slime block, it won't pick up the slime block as well. You must always push the slime block first.

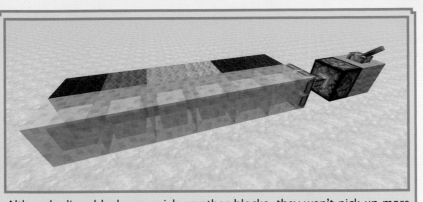

Although slime blocks can pick up other blocks, they won't pick up more than the usual 12-block maximum that a piston can push.

Players and items will bounce when they hit slime blocks.

Despite their appearance, slime blocks don't act like other transparent blocks. You can place torches on the sides of them, and they will also conduct a redstone current if you place redstone dust on them. They will also suffocate mobs.

LIGHTING SYSTEM

You wouldn't think twice about switching on a light in your own home, but in Minecraft even that simple action requires a redstone circuit . . . Creating that circuit is up to you.

 TIP: We suggest that you try out the challenges in this section of the book in Creative mode while you get used to working with redstone. That way you'll have access to all the materials you need and won't have to worry about collecting resources.

DAYLIGHT SENSOR LIGHTING SYSTEM

REDSTONE LAMP RECIPE

You can craft a redstone lamp using redstone dust and glowstone.

DAYLIGHT SENSOR RECIPE

You can craft a daylight sensor from glass, Nether quartz, and wood slabs.

1

Clear a 5x1 opening in your roof. Fill that space with redstone lamps, then place a daylight sensor next to the lamps, with a 1-block space between them. This picture shows the ideal placement.

2

Place a repeater in front of the daylight sensor, facing toward the lamps. Run redstone dust along the redstone lamps to connect them.

3

Hit the Use Item button to change the daylight sensor to night mode. You can tell which mode the sensor is in by its color — in night mode it appears blue, and in day mode it's yellow.

4

The daylight sensor emits a signal of varying strength depending on the light level. The darker it gets, the stronger the signal, but you can use a repeater to extend the signal, allowing you to power your lights at the first sign of darkness.

 DID YOU KNOW? Redstone lamps are conductive blocks, which means they can power adjacent redstone lamps without giving them direct power. Bear this in mind when making larger lighting systems and you'll save yourself some redstone dust.

A beautifully illuminated home and not one switch in sight!

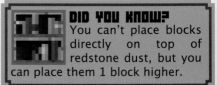

PISTON DOORS

Piston doors are a very popular redstone contraption that open as if by magic, and constructing one is a great way to learn about all the vital elements of redstone.

SLIDING DOOR

TIP: Bear in mind that when you place a sticky piston, its sticky side will be facing toward you.

DID YOU KNOW? You can't place blocks directly on top of redstone dust, but you can place them 1 block higher.

1

Build a 3x3 block arch with a 2-block empty space in the center for the doorway. Then place 2 sticky pistons to the right of the door, facing inward, and place 2 blocks in front of them.

 Redstone creators often use different-colored wool blocks to signal different parts of their circuits. The different-colored wool blocks make it easier to see how the circuits are created, so we have used this method throughout the book.

2

Dig down 2 blocks behind the pistons. Place a block of blue wool in the hole and a redstone torch on top of it to create your NOT gate.

3

Place another block on top of the torch, then place redstone dust on top of that. This dust will be enough to power both of the pistons. Your door's finished!

4

Dig a 2-block-deep trench running from the blue wool block to the front of the door. Run redstone dust along the bottom of the trench right up to the door. This will allow you to connect a pressure plate to the pistons.

::| _T••|| ••••••:

...CONTINUED

5

Fill in the top layer of your trench with blocks of your choice and place a pressure plate in the doorway so the door can be triggered to open. Because of the NOT gate, the pressure plate causes the pistons to open the door instead of closing it, which is far more useful.

6

To make your door open from either side, dig another identical trench from the back of the door to the pistons, and place another pressure plate inside. Now hide your circuitry with extra blocks.

WARNING: A piston door activated by a pressure plate can be a great way to welcome guests to your home, but don't forget that pressure plates can be activated by foes as well! Is that a zombie in the living room?

Uh-oh, ZOMBIES!

MINE CART STATION

Before the introduction of horses, minecarts were the only way to travel in style, and they are still a popular mode of transport. You can use redstone circuits to make minecarts even more exciting.

BASIC MINECART STATION

You will need powered rails and a track switcher to create a basic minecart station. The powered rails get the minecart moving fast, and the track switcher allows you to select your destination station.

MINECART RECIPE

Smelt 5 blocks of iron ore in a furnace to give you 5 iron ingots, which will make a minecart.

RAIL RECIPE

16

16 basic rails can be crafted from a stick and 6 iron ingots.

POWERED RAIL RECIPE

6

You can craft 6 powered rails from a stick, redstone dust, and gold ingots.

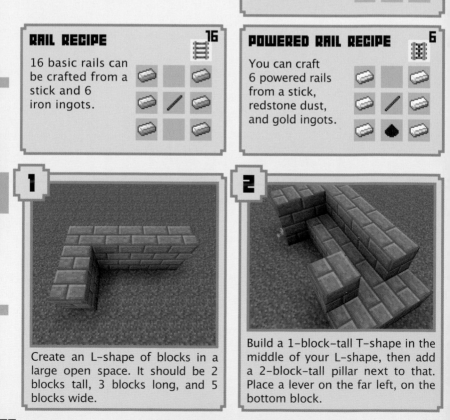

1 Create an L-shape of blocks in a large open space. It should be 2 blocks tall, 3 blocks long, and 5 blocks wide.

2 Build a 1-block-tall T-shape in the middle of your L-shape, then add a 2-block-tall pillar next to that. Place a lever on the far left, on the bottom block.

3

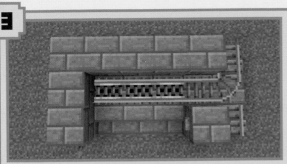

Place a button on the 2-block-tall pillar. You'll be able to reach this from your minecart. Now build a T-junction (a junction where 2 tracks meet) by placing 3 powered rails followed by 4 regular rails. Add stairs leading up to your rails.

4

Dig a trench 1 block below the main curved track. Dig 1 more block down, and fill that space with light-blue wool blocks as shown above. Then add 1 more blue block on top, as shown. Finally, run redstone from behind the lever to the last blue block.

 DID YOU KNOW? At top speed, minecarts move at 8 miles per hour. They will move farther if they are carrying someone or something.

5

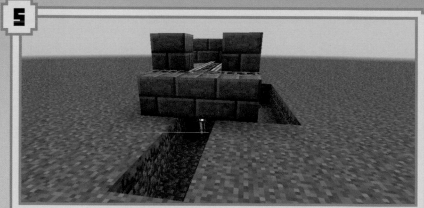

Dig a 1-block-deep trench underneath the junction so you can get to the wool block. Now place a redstone torch on the side of the wool block facing the junction. This torch will act as your signal for switching tracks.

6

Fill in the trench and complete your track so that it has 2 destinations. When you pull your lever, your junction will switch position. Now the fun can begin: Set down your minecart on the rails, get in, push the button, and you're away!

TIP: When you run over a powered rail that is turned off, a frictional force that is usually enough to stop your minecart is applied. You can use powered rails that are turned off to create more stations along your track.

ADVANCED MINECART STATION

One day, with a bit of practice, an advanced station like this could be yours! It has several interesting features: multiple destination selection, selection lights, selection sounds, separate arrival and departure tracks, and a minecart dispenser.

The concept is similar to the basic station in that it uses a power source to switch the T-junctions and select the destination station, but it uses a different button system to allow you to pick your destinaton.

PULSE SHORTENER

T he pulse shortener, or monostable circuit, is one of the mos important logic gates used in complex redstone machines. It allow: you to keep something turned on for a certain amount of time.

DID YOU KNOW? Most power sources in Minecraft have either an indefinite on time (levers) or a fairly long time (buttons). Pulse shorteners allow us to control the amount of time each power source gives.

A pulse shortener is the starting point for many redstone creations. You car use it to control how long a door stays open or how many arrows are fired from a dispenser.

POWERED TRAPDOOR

This example shows a pulse shortener in use with a trapdoor. The circuit is toggled on so that the trapdoor is shut, then when something walks over it, you can flip the switch and the trapdoor will flip open quickly. Gotcha!

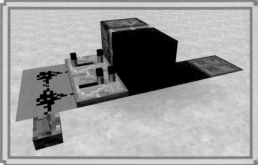

Dig a 2-block-wide hole and fill it with light-green wool. Then place 2 repeaters, facing away from the wool. Set the left repeater to 4 ticks by hitting the Use Item button, and leave the right one set to 1 tick.

Place a sticky piston next to the 4-tick repeater, facing right, and attach a block of blue wool to it as shown.

2

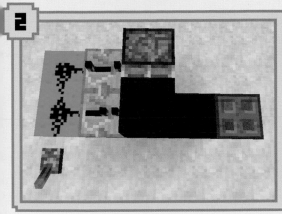

Dig a hole next to the blue wool block and place another blue block in the hole. Place a lever next to the light-green circuit.

Place redstone dust as shown in the image. The circuit in this example is connected to a trapdoor with a hole beneath it, but the choice of mechanism is up to you.

3

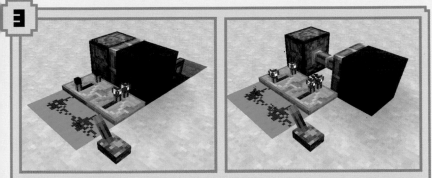

When you pull the lever back to activate the circuit, the trapdoor will open for a short period of time (the exact time will depend on the number of ticks set). Then, when the piston pushes the blue block out, the circuit will be broken and the trapdoor will close again.

In this example the trapdoor opens and shuts quickly. If you add more repeaters on the back row you can keep it open for longer.

TRAPDOOR RECIPE

You can craft 2 trapdoors to catch your enemies, using 6 wood planks.

TOGGLE FLIP-FLOP

No, not that kind of flip-flop! The toggle flip-flop is another important circuit. It provides a redstone signal that can be toggled on and off.

A toggle flip-flop is especially useful when you want to use a button instead of a lever to activate mechanisms like doors.

The example below uses a sticky piston T flip-flop design. What a mouthful! The signal arrives into the circuit, then the flip-flop circuit toggles its output on. If you send another signal to the circuit, it will toggle its output off.

1

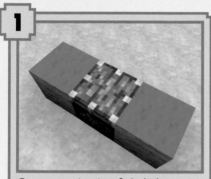

Create a circuit of 2 light-green wool blocks, placed 1 block apart from each other. Place a sticky piston facing upward in the middle of the wool blocks.

2

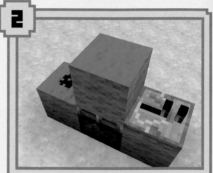

Put another wool block on top of the piston. Then place redstone dust on the block on the left and a repeater facing away from the middle on the block on the right.

3

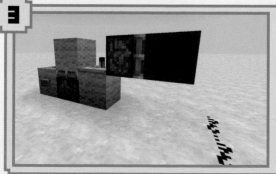

Place a sticky piston (facing right) next to the repeater, 1 block up. (You'll need to place a block below it first, then destroy it.) Attach a block of redstone to the sticky piston. Finally, place a button on the side of the light-green block on the left and dust on the floor, as shown.

4

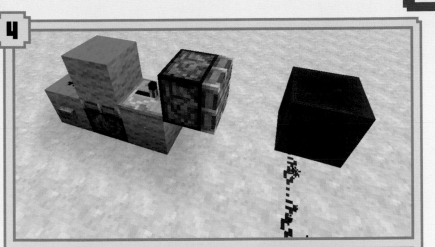

Press the button and the sticky piston on the right will push out the redstone block, powering your redstone wire. Press it again and the piston will pull the block back, disconnecting the circuit.

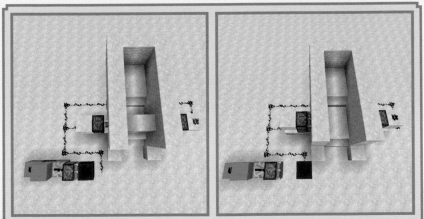

This is a toggle flip-flop being used to power a piston door (as featured on pages 24-25). The flip-flop powers the circuit when it is turned on. And, because it toggles, you don't have to dash through before it slams shut in your face!

CLOCK CIRCUIT

lock circuits are used to create pulsing signals for a variety of machines, from alarms to arrow launchers. It might not sound like the most exciting tool, but it's the starting point for creating some really cool stuff!

REDSTONE TORCH 3-CLOCK

A torch clock is a series of redstone torches strung together that continually turn one another off. The result is a pulsing output signal that switches on and off repeatedly. This example is called a 3-clock, because there are 3 on and 3 off ticks between each pulse. You can make clocks with more torches, but you must always use an odd number of torches in the loop to allow each torch to turn the next torch off before it is turned off itself. If you use an even number of torches, half of the torches will be permanently switched on and the other half permanently off. Not very useful!

1

Find an open space and build this light-green wool circuit. The circuit is made up of 2 blocks with a 2-block trench between them, with 2 blocks filling the trench.

2

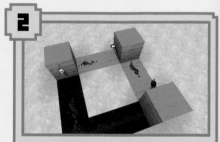

Repeat Step 1 to create another green line as shown above. Add redstone torches, then add a trench of blue blocks to join up the green circuits. Link the torches together with redstone dust.

FROM BASIC 3-CLOCK TO ARROW DISPENSER

You have now built a basic 3-clock. The next steps show you how you can use this circuit to make an arrow dispenser, which is a super-cool and highly useful weapon.

DISPENSER RECIPE

A dispenser can be crafted from 7 cobblestone blocks, 1 redstone dust, and 1 bow.

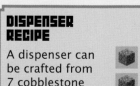

TIMED AUTOMATIC ARROW SHOOTER

3

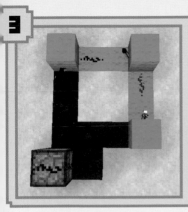

Place a block next to the corner of the blue circuit, then a dispenser on top. Put redstone dust on top of the dispenser. (See the tip below.) Now place another single block next to the dispenser with redstone dust on top to link the circuit.

TIP: As with a sticky piston, when you place a dispenser it will be facing toward you. Make sure you're facing in the opposite direction to the way you want it to dispense.

4

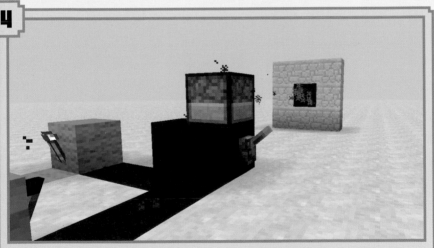

Put a lever on the side of one of the blue blocks to turn the circuit on and off. Fill the dispenser with arrows, hit the lever, and let 'em fly!

Players of the PC/Mac Edition will discover that it isn't possible to put redstone on a dispenser simply by right-clicking on it, as this will open the dispenser. Hold down Shift as you right-click to place redstone dust. Hold Shift and Space to perform this while flying.

CLOCK CIRCUITS
...CONTINUED

REPEATER CLOCK

A repeater clock is made of 2 repeaters passing a signal around in a constant loop. To prevent the repeaters simply powering each other on, it is started by a 1-tick signal from a pulse

shortener, which ensures the repeaters are only on for 1 tick before turning off again. They pass the signal around in a loop while continually turning on and off, which means your arrow dispenser will now pack some serious fire-power. Enemies, beware!

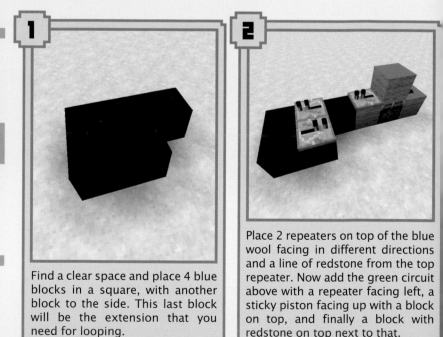

1

Find a clear space and place 4 blue blocks in a square, with another block to the side. This last block will be the extension that you need for looping.

2

Place 2 repeaters on top of the blue wool facing in different directions and a line of redstone from the top repeater. Now add the green circuit above with a repeater facing left, a sticky piston facing up with a block on top, and finally a block with redstone on top next to that.

3

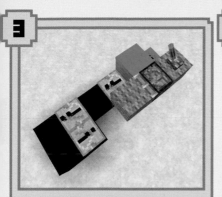

To add the toggle, create the floating pink circuit next to the highest green block. Place a sticky piston facing left (toward the repeaters), a block on the back with a lever on top, and a block in front.

4

Add a staircase of blocks in front of the 2 repeaters. Place a dispenser on the top and add redstone dust as before. This completes the circuit.

5

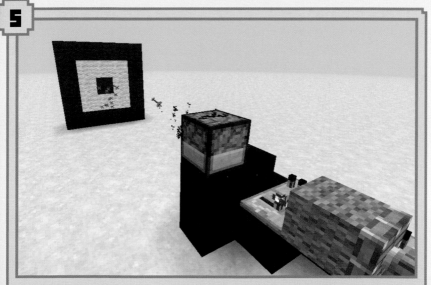

Add plenty of arrows to your dispenser. Pull the lever and the arrows will shoot out incredibly fast. This one is guaranteed to scare your enemies away!

DELUXE LIGHTING SYSTEM

This seriously cool lighting system doesn't just turn your lights on and off, it physically moves the light source in and out of the room using a block swapper. A challenging build, but great fun and well worth the effort.

CONSTRUCTION MATERIALS

Switched off/switched on

1

Clear a space above your selected room. It will need to be at least 5x3 blocks. The light will sit flush with the ceiling so you won't have to change the way the ceiling looks. You'll just need to make a hole in the ceiling where you would like the glowstone light to appear when you turn the switch on.

2

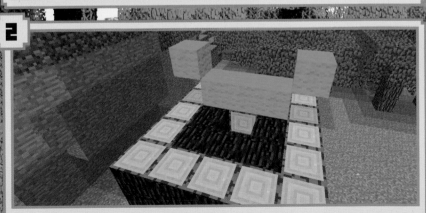

Place 3 light-green wool blocks in a row, just behind your hole, then add an extra block at a diagonal at each end.

3

Add a redstone torch on top of the central green wool block, and place 2 repeaters on either side of this torch. They should be pointing away from the torch and directed into the 2 blocks at either end. Now add a redstone torch to the side of these 2 blocks (not on top).

4

Place a regular piston directly below the redstone torch on the left, so that it faces the hole in the ceiling. Then add a sticky piston 1 block above the ceiling, facing down toward the hole, so that the blocks can slide past it before being pushed into the roof. This can be tricky to place, so place 3 blocks above the hole, then remove the lowest 2. Jump down the hole, look upward, and place your sticky piston on the underside of the green wool.

Add a regular ceiling material block to the right of the sticky piston, then fill the hole in the ceiling with a glowstone block, ensuring it touches the sticky piston face. Then add one more piston facing toward the regular ceiling material block.

Decide where you'd like the on/off switch to sit inside the room and place either a lever or a button there. Remember to connect your lever/button to the main circuit. Try this vertical torch circuit to save on resources.

AUTOMATED CHICKEN FARM

This automated chicken farm produces chicken and feathers, even when you aren't there to operate it. It also has a selection mode that changes the output from cooked chicken to raw chicken.

CONSTRUCTION MATERIALS

1

Position a chest centrally at the front of your allocated area and a hopper facing into the chest — this will collect the chicken and feathers and feed them into the collection chest. Place a light-green wool block 3 blocks back from the hopper. Add a dispenser facing in toward the hopper but 1 block higher. (Place a block under the dispenser first, then remove it.) Now put a cauldron on top of the hopper.

2

Add another light-green wool block behind the dispenser. Put redstone dust on the light-green wool block at the very back. Position a hopper on top of the dispenser. Position a comparator facing away from it and into a third light-green wool block. This will power the redstone dust when it detects that a chicken has laid an egg.

AUTOMATED CHICKEN FARM
...CONTINUED

3

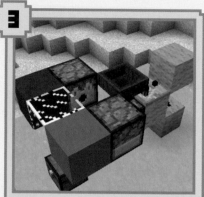

Position 2 dispensers facing into the vacant air block directly in front of the highest hopper. Place red-stained clay, glass, and blue-stained clay across the front of the build as shown.

4

Add buttons to the red and blue blocks. Put a water bucket in the dispenser next to the blue block and a lava bucket in the dispenser next to the red block, then position a cauldron on top of the uppermost hopper.

5

Place a stone slab just above the cauldron. It must be in the top half of the block so there is a gap between the cauldron rim and the slab, so place 2 blocks on top of the cauldron, remove the lower block, position the slab on the underside of the upper block, then remove the upper block. Add 3 more glass blocks. Add 2 more clay blocks, 1 underneath each dispenser.

6

Fill the cauldron with chickens. In Creative mode, you can throw chicken spawn eggs into the cauldron. In Survival, this is best done by collecting regular chicken eggs and throwing them into the cauldron (PC/Mac users, select the eggs in your hotbar and right click to throw). Don't add them too fast, as you might knock some chickens out of the cauldron. Now go about your day, and when you return to your farm, the chest will be full of chicken and feathers.

Press the button on the blue block for raw chicken and the button on the red block for cooked!

CLASSIC JEB DOOR

Despite its name, the Jeb Door wasn't actually created by Jeb himself. Jeb (Jens Bergensten) is the lead developer of Minecraft and he discovered this design on the Internet when pistons first went live in-game.

The design has changed dramatically over time but the basic idea is still the same. The door is hidden from view when closed and sits flush with the wall. When activated it slides across to reveal a secret passageway.

CONSTRUCTION MATERIALS

Find a location for your door. This example uses a cliff, inside which you will create a hidden room. Now decide how you would like to open the door. There are several options, but the simplest way is to use a lever hidden nearby and connected to the door.

2

Place the lever at your chosen location. For the door itself, you will need an area 6 blocks wide, 4 tall, and at least 3 blocks deep. If you can make your space deeper, you'll find it easier to install your door.

3

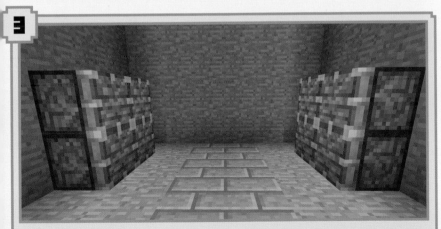

Establish the center of your space and create a 2x4 block pathway down the middle, using stone brick. Place 4 sticky pistons on each side of your space in a 2x2 formation, as shown above, with 4 blocks of space between the pistons on each side. These pistons will slide the door aside once it's been pulled back from the wall.

4

Now place 2 more sticky pistons on each side; they should be facing out toward the front of the clear area and stacked on top of each other. Place a block in front of each of these pistons. Make sure these blocks are the same material as the wall (smooth stone in this case).

5

Place a blue wool block above each piston, and two more in the middle. Then place a repeater on each side facing outward. Make sure each repeater is set to a 2-, 3-, or 4-tick delay — 1 tick won't work. Place redstone dust on top of the remaining blocks to connect the pistons together.

6

Test the system by placing a lever near to the middle and turning it on. The door should extend out into the cliff wall and sit flush against it. After testing, remove the temporary lever. (You will be using the hidden lever that was placed in Step 2.)

7

Your lever now needs to be connected to the redstone on the door. Just run a redstone dust wire from the door to the lever. Make sure the wire is connected in the central area at the top of the door. This ensures that both sides of the door are powered.

Finally, cover up the door mechanism. You can then build a room, a base, or anything else you like behind your very own secret entrance!

LAVA PIT TRAP

This trap is difficult to spot, reacts extremely quickly, and is almost impossible to escape from! It works by pulling the floor out from beneath another player when they open your trapped chest, then it drops them into a pool of lava. *Ouch!*

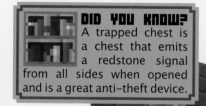
DID YOU KNOW? A trapped chest is a chest that emits a redstone signal from all sides when opened and is a great anti-theft device.

CONSTRUCTION MATERIALS

TRAPPED CHEST RECIPE

A single trapped chest can be crafted from a chest and a trip-wire hook. Place 2 trapped chests next to each other to create a large trapped chest.

1

This trap needs a small corridor, below which the pit will be hidden. Dig your corridor at least 5 blocks long, 2 wide, and 3 tall.

Dig your lava pit. It should be 3x2 blocks and 3 blocks deep. Add a large trapped chest to the end of the corridor. It will need to sit on 2 blocks.

2

At this point, you'll need to temporarily destroy the walls of the corridor to build the redstone mechanics. To create the sliding floor, place 3 sticky pistons on each side of the pit, as shown.

LAVA PIT TRAP
...CONTINUED

3

Now put blocks in front of the pistons; these will be the floor of the corridor. In this example we've used stone brick to help blend the trap into its surroundings.

Place a blue wool block above each sticky piston and then run redstone along the tops. This will power all the pistons on each side so they slide out simultaneously.

4

To connect the chest, dig down 1 block on either side of it so that you can see the blocks on which the chest is sitting. You now need to place redstone torches on the sides of the blocks the chest is on.

5

Hide the torches with stone blocks (the torches will power them, and the floor will slide back into place). To connect that power to the pistons, place a block of wool next to the stone block and put redstone dust on top of both of them (on both sides).

6

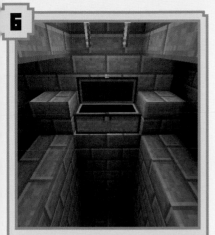

Test your trap by standing in the corridor and opening the chest — you should fall into the pit.

7

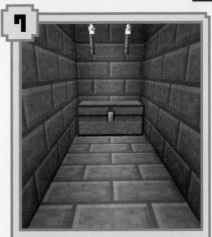

Finally, fill the pit with lava and build up the walls of the corridor to hide the redstone.

The next person who tries to steal your stuff is in for a scorching surprise!

DUAL SHOT CANNON

This cannon fires 2 TNT projectiles at your enemies at the touch of a button. It also allows you to select one of four possible ranges for each shot. Redstone signals are used to activate the required number of TNT dispensers depending on which button you have pressed, releasing a different amount of propellant TNT for each range.

CONSTRUCTION MATERIALS

1

Build a U-shape of light-green wool 6 blocks long and 3 wide, leaving a 1-block space at the back. Place redstone dust on top of each block to create a wire.

2

Starting at the front, place 4 light-green wool blocks in the center of the U-shape but raised 1 block higher. This will eventually be the water bed. Now add 1 red and 1 light-green block to the back of the cannon as shown. Place a redstone torch on top of the red wool and redstone dust on top of the light-green wool.

3

Build an L-shape of red, gray, white, and black wool, positioned a block higher than the red wool with the redstone torch attached to it. Place a ladder on the inside of the red wool at the top of the L-shape. Since ladders occupy an entire block, this will act as a rest point for the TNT projectiles and will stop the water from spilling out.

WOOL SHOT CANNON
...CONTINUED

4

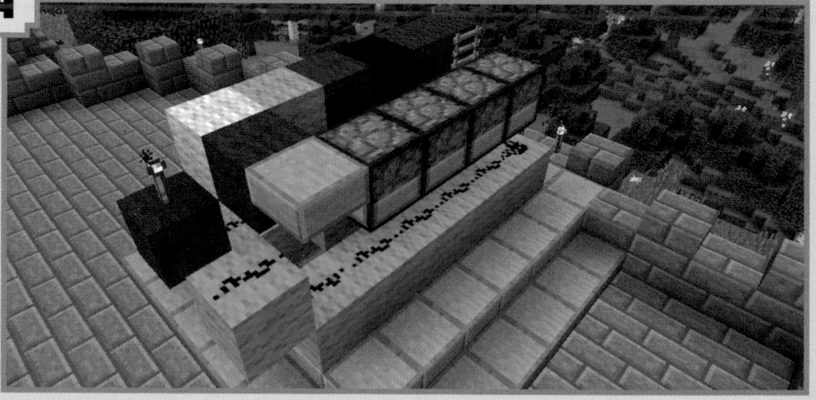

Add a single stone slab to the end of the L-shape as shown. Aim for the top half of the red wool when placing the slab. Now add 4 dispensers opposite the longest side of the L-shape, facing in toward the water bed. These will dispense TNT into the cannon.

5

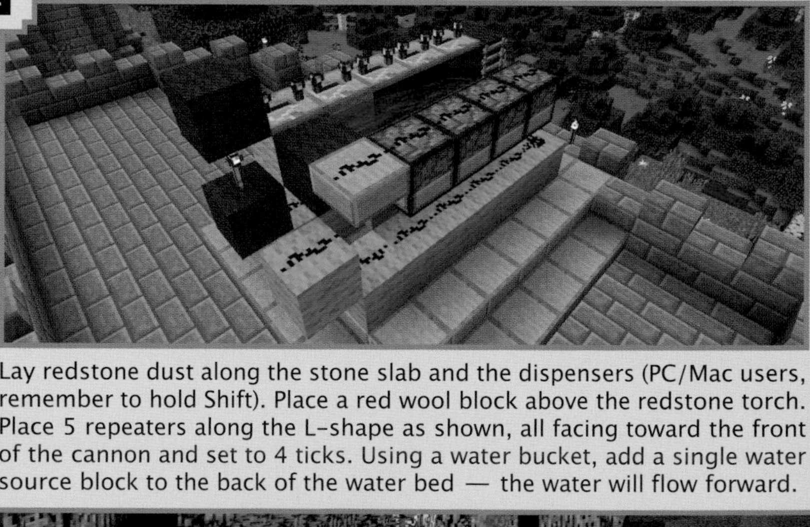

Lay redstone dust along the stone slab and the dispensers (PC/Mac users, remember to hold Shift). Place a red wool block above the redstone torch. Place 5 repeaters along the L-shape as shown, all facing toward the front of the cannon and set to 4 ticks. Using a water bucket, add a single water source block to the back of the water bed — the water will flow forward.

Place the water here.

6

Add 2 dispensers to the top of the wool block with the ladder attached, both facing in toward the water bed. Now add 2 stone slabs as shown, and place 2 red wool blocks on top of these slabs. This will leave you with a single block of air in front of the 2 projectile dispensers.

7

Fill all 6 dispensers with TNT and add 4 range selector buttons along the side of the cannon. Pressing the button on the black block will allow you to fire TNT the farthest, and the button on the white block will fire it the shortest distance. Have fun experimenting with range!

SUPERCHARGED FIRE ARROW LAUNCHER

This amazing machine allows you to shoot flaming arrows out of a dispenser at a rate of 5 per second, at the mere press of a button. That should keep those hostile mobs at bay!

CONSTRUCTION MATERIALS

"Is it just me, or is it getting hot in here?"

1

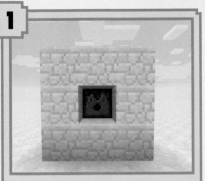

Create a 3x3 square of blocks of your choice, with a 1-block space in the middle. Place another block behind the square in the center, and place a dispenser on top of that. Make sure it's facing in the direction you want to fire.

2

Place a fence gate in front of the hole. You'll need to place another block below it first, then destroy that block when the gate is in place. Hit the Use Item button to open the gate. It doesn't matter whether the fence gate opens inward or outward.

3

The gate acts like a solid block and will allow you to fill the hole with lava without it spilling out of the front.

Place the lava here.

TNT **WARNING:** Adding the lava can be tricky: Make sure you place the lava behind the fence gate and aim for the spot marked in the image. Be especially careful if you're playing in Survival mode. If you pour lava all over yourself, you're going to have a meltdown . . .

SUPERCHARGED FIRE ARROW LAUNCHER

...CONTINUED

4

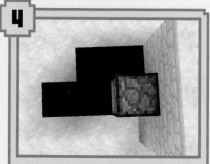

To make the arrows fire from the dispenser at high speed you'll need a super-fast clock circuit. Place 4 blocks on the level below the dispenser as shown.

5

Add redstone dust at each end and 2 repeaters in the middle: one facing into the dispenser and the other facing the opposite way. This forms the clock circuit.

6

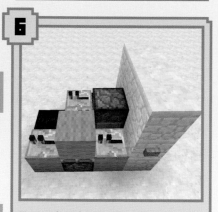

To make the circuit turn on and off at the push of the button, you need a simple piston-based pulse shortener, as shown in green. Then add the button onto the side of the frame.

7

Next, add 4 pink blocks: 2 blocks should be placed at ground level at a diagonal to each other, and 2 more blocks 1 level above the ground, also positioned at a diagonal to each other.

Place redstone dust on the ground-level pink block farthest from the dispenser and a redstone repeater on the other ground-level pink block (facing toward the dispenser). Add a sticky piston to the side of the pink circuit as shown, then add a single pink wool block in front of that sticky piston. Finally, fill your dispenser with arrows, then hit the button, and you're away! Just hit the button again when you want to turn it off.

Arrow launchers positioned behind the walls of a fort. Nobody's getting in here ...

X :-1 T•"II •••••••

The 3x3 piston door is one of the most popular contraptions in the Minecraft community. It's a great addition to any player's base, providing a stylish entrance and access at the touch of a button.

This piston door circulates an item in a loop each time you directly power the bottom left dropper with either a repeater, button, or lever. This is a handy, compact way of creating an on/off toggle for contraptions.

CONSTRUCTION MATERIALS

1

Build a 5x5 stone brick frame for the door ensuring you have 3 blocks of space below for the hopper/dropper T flip-flop. Create a loop out of 3 droppers and a hopper below the frame as shown, each facing in the direction indicated by the arrows. Add a repeater facing in toward the flip-flop on top of a light-green wool block and a comparator pointing away from the flip-flop on top of a light-blue wool block, as shown.

2

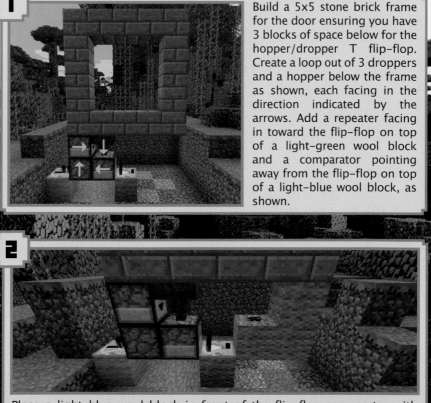

Place a light-blue wool block in front of the flip-flop comparator with redstone dust on top. Add another light-blue wool block next to this block, then place a third light-blue wool block on top of this.

▖▘ ▗▖▀▛▘▞ ▙▙▀▜

...CONTINUED

3

Add a redstone torch to the side of the highest light-blue wool block as shown. Place another light-blue wool block 2 blocks below the redstone torch and then place redstone dust on top of it. The dust should power the torch straight away.

4

Place another light-blue wool block above the redstone torch, with another redstone torch on top. Above this redstone torch (now off) place a block with redstone dust on it. Add 3 wool blocks on top of the frame and run redstone dust along the top.

5

Position 2 more redstone torches as shown. They should both be pointing in toward what will eventually be the rest of the door.

Imagine the powered redstone dust takes up an entire block of space directly above it. Now place a light-blue wool block to the side of the powered redstone dust and put a sticky piston on top of this. It should face inward, toward the center of the build. Place another wool block on the end of the extended piston arm. Add another inward-facing sticky piston above the extended piston arm — aim for the brown top side of the piston face when placing.

Place a red wool block 2 blocks below the light-blue block at the end of the extended piston. Place a repeater on top of that block, facing in to the center of the build. This should be set to 4 ticks.

Position 2 upward-facing sticky pistons in the center of the build. The first one should be next to the repeater set to 4 ticks and the second should be next to the blue wool block on the end of the currently extended sticky piston.

9

Place a red wool block on the side of the lowest sticky piston. Lay a repeater on top, facing in toward the piston and set to 4 ticks. Add 2 more red wool blocks as shown and run redstone dust on top of them.

10

Fill in the second layer of stone bricks. Follow the current frame layout, but leave out the bottom 2 corners, which are occupied by a piston and the redstone dust on top of the red wool.

11

Add the remaining sticky pistons as shown, facing inward. Add blocks above each set of 2 pistons on each side of the frame, then run redstone dust along the top. All 7 pistons are now connected to 1 redstone wire and will operate at the same time when the circuit is activated.

12

Add another inward-facing sticky piston to the side of the light-blue block that's powering the extended piston. Place a redstone block at the end of the extended sticky piston arm. Place a red wool block to the side and 1 block below the redstone block. Add redstone dust — it should immediately be powered by the redstone block.

13

Place an upward-facing sticky piston next to the block with the powered redstone on top. Put a block on top of the extended piston arm. Place another block to the right of the piston, with a repeater on top, facing away from the piston and left on 1 tick. This repeater should connect to an adjacent block with redstone dust on top of it, 1 block higher up.

14

Add a block of your choosing to the dropper underneath the hopper. Add the final layer of the frame at the front and run a line of redstone from the bottom left dropper at the front to the spot where you'd like the button to be. You now have a stylish, secret entrance!

POTION LAB

This lab allows you to brew potions simply by pressing a few buttons. You can use the control panel to select which type of potion is brewed, and which modifiers are added. Magic!

CONSTRUCTION MATERIALS

DIFFICULTY ■■■

1

Build a 4x2 rectangle for the potion modifier panel (you'll need 2 blocks below for the mechanisms). Use cyan-, purple-, red-, and yellow-stained clay in the formation shown. Place 4 buttons down the left side of the panel. Pair each button with an item frame on the right. Starting from the top, place the following items into the item frames: gunpowder, fermented spider eye, redstone dust, and glowstone dust.

2

Build the water bottle feeding system next to the potion modifier panel. Place a brewing stand as shown, with a hopper directly above it to feed the ingredients into the brewing stand. Finally, place 2 light-blue-stained clay blocks above the hopper. Label the top block with a water bottle in an item frame.

3

Place a hopper on the side of the brewing stand. Make sure it's facing into the stand as it will feed water bottles from chests above. Place a chest, a hopper, and another chest in a vertical stack above this hopper. Fill the top chest with water bottles. The bottles will immediately disappear as they travel down through the system.

POTION LAB
...CONTINUED

4

Now build your 5x4 base ingredient panel using lime-green and green-stained clay. This is where you'll select the potion you want to brew. Arrange the buttons as shown — 5 along the very bottom row, and 5 along the second row from the top.

5

Pair each button with an item frame. Rename the items listed below, using an anvil, so that players can see their function when they hover over them in their item frames. Then, starting at the top left and working across, fill each item frame with the renamed items.

TOP ROW		BOTTOM ROW	
	Leaping		Poison
	Fire resistance		Night vision
	Swiftness		Regeneration
	Water breathing		Strength
	Healing		Weakness

6

Build the light-green wool circuit underneath the ingredient panel — you'll need 5 blocks in total. Run redstone dust along the 4 light-green wool blocks that sit in a row.

Place the light-blue wool block as shown. It should be 1 block below and behind the green panel, in line with the end column. Place redstone dust on top. Place a line of 4 droppers facing upward next to the redstone. As you look at the back of the lab, from left to right the droppers should be filled with blaze powder, ghast tears, golden carrots, and spider eyes.

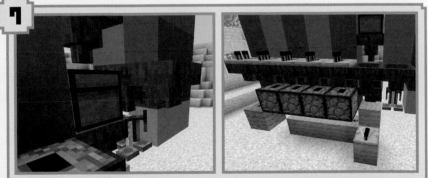

7

Place another hopper feeding into the ingredient hopper above the brewing stand. From here, create a chain of 6 hoppers all facing in the same direction as the first. Place 5 repeaters on top of the hoppers as shown (PC and Mac users will need to hold Shift while doing so), making sure they are facing away from the control panel and are set to 1 tick. Find the light-green wool block situated under the lowest hopper, and run a repeater away from it, placed on top of another light-green wool block.

POTION LAB
...CONTINUED

8

Place another light-green wool block 1 block below and behind the glowstone button, then place redstone dust on top. Stack 3 droppers above the redstone dust, facing in to the center of the lab. Place a dropper next to the redstone dust, facing upward. Above this, place a hopper facing into the first hopper you placed in Step 7. Stack 2 hoppers above this, both feeding down. Add the modifier panel ingredients to the 4 droppers on the right. Starting from the top, these are gunpowder, fermented spider eye, redstone dust, and glowstone dust.

9

Add 5 droppers facing into the chain of hoppers, across from the row of repeaters. Fill these droppers with the following ingredients, from left to right as you look at the back of the lab: glistering melon, pufferfish, sugar, magma cream, and rabbit's feet. Place a row of clay blocks along the top of the 5 droppers. Add another light-blue wool block to the existing blue circuit (bottom left) and place redstone on top.

10

Place a light-green wool block in front of the lowest repeater, but a block higher up, and redstone dust on top of that. Place another light-green wool block to the side of the redstone dust, with a dropper on top facing into the hopper chain. Fill this dropper with Nether wart. Add a light-blue wool block to the side of the middle dropper in the stack of 3 as shown.

Attach a row of 5 stone slabs to the back of the 5 droppers (aim for the upper half of the droppers). Place 5 repeaters on top of the stone slabs, facing away from the control panel. Place 8 light-green wool blocks behind the repeaters and connect them to the dropper containing the Nether wart using redstone. Connect the 2 blue wool blocks at either end with a line of blue wool. Add redstone dust to all but the final blue block next to the hoppers. Now press the required button on the modifier panel, then press the necessary button on the ingredient panel to create your first potion. See the Combat Handbook for a list of potion recipes.

14 FLOOR ELEVATOR

The 14 Floor Elevator created by Cubehamster is one of the most impressive single-task redstone contraptions ever made. It allows you to travel to 14 different floors in a super-fast piston elevator. Now, that's traveling redstone style!

The player accesses a user interface at each level to select which floor they want, in much the same way as a real elevator.

CUBEHAMSTER: This well-respected redstone expert is a teacher of physics and chemistry based in the Netherlands. He's never been known to turn down a challenge!

PISTON ELEVATOR

The concept behind the moving part of the elevator is pretty simple. The design is 2 blocks wide, and the player needs to stand right in the middle of 2 pistons. The player is pushed up by a piston on the left, then a piston on the right, and this process is repeated until they reach the desired floor.

This concept was originally showcased by the player Brows of Steel and has since become the standard mechanism for many piston elevators.

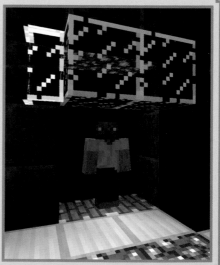

1[illegible] . L[illegible] L[illegible] TU[illegible]
...CONTINUED

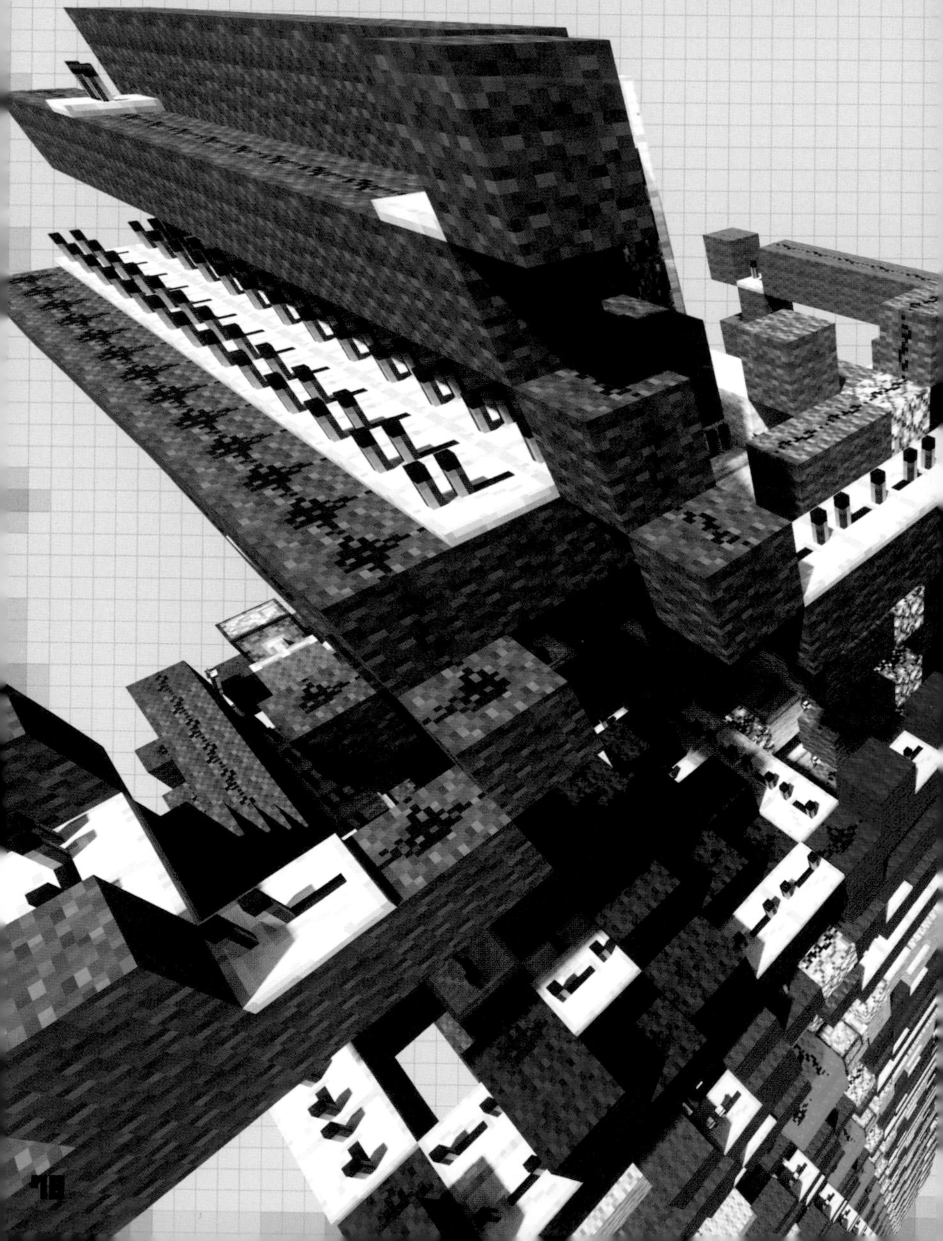

FLOOR SELECTION

Although the moving elevator part is simple, the circuitry that allows you to select a floor is a whole new level of complicated!

Like a real elevator, there is a different button to press for each floor. Each button sends a redstone signal when pressed. These signals vary in length depending on which button they have come from, so the elevator can figure out which floor has been chosen by detecting the length of the signal.

INSTANT CALL FUNCTION

One of the best things about this elevator is that the player doesn't have to wait for the elevator to arrive at their floor. In fact, it's quicker than elevators in the real world. When the player selects a floor by pressing a button, the signal is sent directly to the floor that he's on and the elevator is immediately ready for use.

SUMMARY

In version 1.5.2, this piston elevator was the pinnacle of elevator design. None could match its speed and efficiency. Although this design was too big and too complicated to create in a Survival game, Cubehamster also created a simpler, more practical elevator design that transported a player one floor at a time. He really did think of everything!

COLOR MAP DISPLAY

Y ou can't tell at first glance, but this enormous redstone contraption creates an image so large that it can only be viewed on a Minecraft map.

SETHBLING: Before he discovered Minecraft, Seth was a software engineer at Microsoft.

For more creations from SethBling check out: **www.youtube.com/sethbling**

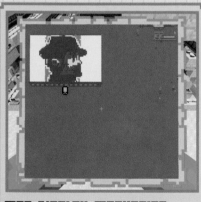

MAP DISPLAY MECHANICS

The map figures out which color occurs most often within each 2x2 block area, and uses that dominant color for 1 pixel. Viewed from above, the machine has 1 wood and 1 stone block in each cell. The redstone pushes 2 more blocks into play, and that determines the color of the pixel. When you look at the Color Map Display on a map you'll see it's formed an image, like this one of Notch. Amazing!

PISTON PIXEL CHANGERS

You can program several different images into the machine. Devices called piston loops arrange blocks in the display area until the image has been prepared. It can then be viewed on a map. You can change the image at the push of a button: When you hit it, the piston loops push new blocks into place and the new image is ready to view on your map.

REDSTONE

It's the redstone's job to shift all of the piston loops around at the same time. This is done from a single button!

JL2579 TIMEWATCH

This super stopwatch created by JL2579 and Cubehamster is an amazing piece of redstone engineering. It can record time to an accuracy of a 10th of a second. Blink and you'll miss it!

It uses a super-fast memory array to measure the time and a compact decoder system to display the numbers on a 4-digit display. It has 2 buttons, one to start and stop the timer, and one to reset the time after it has been used and recorded.

JL2579: JL specializes in amazing redstone and piston creations, as well as big farms. He's particularly interested in pushing the boundaries of what's possible in Survival mode to their very limits.

For more creations from JL2579 check out:
www.youtube.com/JL2579

SUPER-FAST REPEATER LOCK MEMORY ARRAY

The driving force behind this stopwatch is a unique memory system, which is used to store and record the numbers that are then displayed on the 4-digit display.

This system uses the repeater lock function. When you hit the Stop button, the repeaters lock the time that is currently on the display. When you hit the button again, the clock continues from that time. The repeater lock can process information very quickly. This is essential for a stopwatch since it is recording units of time smaller than 1 second.

DID YOU KNOW? This kind of clock display is called a 7-segment display. Much like an LED clock in the real world that has 7 LED segments for each number, this clock has 7 redstone lamp segments for each number.

...CONTINUED

DECODER

The special memory array needs a special decoder to display the numbers using redstone lamp segments. This clever redstone component uses what's known as a *slide system* to display different numbers.

The slide system pushes sets of blocks (arranged vertically to save space) into the path of constantly powered repeaters. When a block that allows a redstone signal to pass through it is pushed into place, the signal from the repeater is sent down a line of redstone that goes directly into the back of the corresponding segment of the display and lights it up.

But this system has one small drawback: Because the slide system then has to be pushed back up into its default position, it can't change state fast enough to keep up with the superfast repeater lock memory array that drives it. So the 10ths of each second are only displayed after the Stop button is pressed.

SUMMARY

JL's stopwatch is a fantastic example of a high-end redstone machine. The concept isn't unique, but the way in which it delivers its timekeeping is. This is one of the most compact stopwatches ever created.

DID YOU KNOW? Stopwatches like this one have been used in numerous mini-games and adventure maps to time laps and tasks set during the adventure. Check out FVDisco's Sonic the Hedgehog™ map — it's a great example.

GOLD RUSH

old Rush is a redstone mini-game that's big on fun! The idea is to control a villager in a minecart, leading him to several chutes to collect gold bars, while avoiding the TNT that also drops into the chutes. It's explosive fun!

The player stands on a platform and moves a minecart by stepping on and off a pressure plate. You can change the direction of the track using a lever. You can choose to play one of three levels of difficulty: TNT can fall in either one, two, or three of the four lanes.

CNB: aka Nick Farwell, is based in the UK and is well respected for his redstone tutorials.

PISTON LOOPS AND 7-SEGMENT DISPLAY SCOREBOARD

All the game information is stored in a piston loop. This is a selection of blocks that is continually moved around by pistons. The blocks turn redstone lamps on or off, depending on which type of block is in play: glass or a solid block. Glass doesn't allow a redstone signal to pass through it and so gives an off state, whereas a solid block does allow the signal through, resulting in an on state.

TIP: If you want to get high scores, play on the highest level of difficulty.

GOLD RUSH
...CONTINUED

REDSTONE RANDOMIZER

This machine is used to randomize the chutes that the gold and TNT fall into, and it does this by detecting when a chicken runs onto a pressure plate!

Every time a chicken activates a pressure plate, the plate emits a signal that is sent to a piston loop that controls which chutes the TNT/gold drops into. It takes several chickens inside the randomizer to generate a high number and a variety of drops from the chutes.

SUMMARY

The mechanism behind Gold Rush is a tangle of piston loops and logic gates. It uses clocks, pulse shorteners, AND gates, NOT gates, transistors, and T flip-flops!

It's a complex design, but when you break it down, it's simply a collection of common redstone components that have been linked in an incredibly clever way to create an awesome redstone machine.

ZOMBIE SIEGE

Zombie Siege is a fun combat mini-game. The player must defend his or her base from hordes of zombies that are lumbering toward it by firing at them with a bow and arrows and TNT cannons. Who said a zombie apocalypse couldn't be fun?

The first few rounds are a nice, easy warm-up for the player, but once you hit double digits, the difficulty rapidly ramps up. At this point your cannon aim has to be right on target if you want to survive.

TNT CANNONS

You can set the TNT cannon to 3 different ranges, allowing you to blow up zombies virtually anywhere on the map. They are controlled by 3 buttons (one for each range). Cleverly, they use the same piece of redstone dust to carry their separate signals; by placing each button 1 block farther away from the cannon, the machine can work out how far the signal has traveled and, therefore, which button has been pressed. Depending on which button it is, the game loads different amounts of propellant TNT into the cannon to control the range of the block of TNT that's actually being fired.

DID YOU KNOW? In order to keep the zombies from catching fire in the sun for this game, FVDisco had to construct an enormous sheet of ice and position it in the sky above.

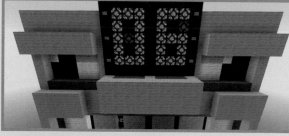

7-SEGMENT LEVEL DISPLAY

The level display shows you which round of the game you're currently playing. There are 99 rounds in total, but nobody has ever made it that far!

ZOMBIE CONTROLLER

As in Gold Rush, the zombies are spawned randomly by a chicken walking over a pressure plate, which sends a signal to a dispenser and a mob egg. The number of dispensers increases with each level you pass, meaning there are more zombies to kill.

To encourage the zombies to walk in the right direction, Disco uses villagers in minecarts under the floor! Zombies can sense targets through solid blocks even if they can't see them, and will head for the villagers.

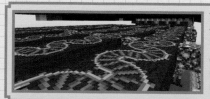

The minecarts carrying the villagers need to move fairly slowly so that the zombies don't lose interest. Disco uses wiggly tracks to slow the minecarts down.

SUMMARY

Zombie Siege uses a combination of TNT cannons and traditional weaponry, along with huge waves of marauding zombies to create an awesome mini-game.

The redstone circuitry behind the game involves some imaginative techniques. The variable range cannon was one of the first to be made and used in a game so successfully. The simple single-range version has since become the standard design for TNT cannons.

HINT AND TIPS

We spoke to the experts themselves to get their tips on working with redstone. Here's what the Mojang team had to say:

- Working with redstone can be frustrating, but stick to it! It's very satisfying to see your creation function as intended after all your hard work.

- If your redstone creation includes TNT, wait until everything else is placed before placing the TNT. It's far less dangerous that way.

- Try testing out your designs in Creative mode before making them in Survival.

- Building is more fun with friends. Your parents might come in handy, too!

- Focus on getting your creations to work properly before making them more compact or more attractive.

- We're still adding new features! Just because you can't do something now, doesn't mean you won't be able to do it in the future.

- Do not build redstone creations next to water. It'll mess up your plans!

USEFUL LINKS

Check out this list of useful websites. They'll really extend your Minecrafting experience.

Official Minecraft website:
http://minecraft.net

Official Mojang website:
http://mojang.com

The Minecraft wiki:
www.minecraftwiki.net

The official Facebook page:
www.facebook.com/minecraft

Mojang Team's YouTube channel:
www.youtube.com/teammojang

The official Minecraft Twitter page:
https://twitter.com/Mojang

Notch's official Twitter page:
https://twitter.com/notch

Jeb's official Twitter page:
https://twitter.com/jeb_

Here are some other Minecraft sites, not monitored by Mojang or Scholastic. Enter at your own risk!

Creative community fansite Planet Minecraft:
www.planetminecraft.com

The Skindex — for all your Minecraft fashion needs:
www.minecraftskins.com

Minecraft on Reddit:
www.reddit.com/r/Minecraft/

Disco's YouTube channel:
www.youtube.com/FVDisco

SethBling's YouTube channel:
www.youtube.com/sethbling

JL2579's YouTube channel:
www.youtube.com/JL2579

(See the copyright page for our Stay Safe Online policy.)